Original title:
The Orchard of Wonders

Copyright © 2025 Creative Arts Management OÜ
All rights reserved.

Author: Oliver Bennett
ISBN HARDBACK: 978-1-80586-383-0
ISBN PAPERBACK: 978-1-80586-855-2

Gardens of Whimsy and Wonder

In the garden where the gnomes all dance,
The squirrels wear hats and prance with chance.
Flowers bloom in checkerboard shoes,
While rabbits play cards, they've nothing to lose.

The bees hum tunes of a jazzy spree,
While the funky toad sings in harmony.
Worms throw a party, with soil as the stage,
As the moon takes a bow, it's quite the rage!

Grappling with the Essence of Life

Carrots debate the meaning of fate,
While potatoes play chess and contemplate.
A confused tomato thought he was a berry,
But found out the truth made him feel quite hairy.

A cucumber slick, with shades so bright,
Wears a frown, but looks quite alright.
As radishes giggle and sprout their legs,
Life's silly moments are what it begs!

Celestial Fruits and Earthly Joys

Peaches wear crowns in the backyard of bliss,
While apricots tango, who could miss?
Melons in moonlight play hide and seek,
With laughter so loud, it makes the trees creak.

The berries gossip under leafy wraps,
While citrus makes puns that are quite a snap.
In this fruity fiesta, all worries dissapate,
As laughter and sweetness celebrate fate!

A Haven for the Dreamers

In a nook where the daisies have tea every night,
Dreamers converse with stars, oh, what a sight!
Clouds wear pajamas and drift on by,
While crickets crack jokes that make fireflies cry.

The trees spin tales of the wildest dreams,
As the moon juggles wonders, or so it seems.
With laughter echoing through the shimmering leaves,
A haven for dreamers, oh, how it weaves!

The Garden of Unseen Dreams

In a garden where daisies grow,
The squirrels dance in quite a show.
They wear tiny hats made of leaves,
Peddling lemonade mixed with peas.

The violets gossip, it's true,
While the snails race under skies so blue.
With each twist of a funky breeze,
The cucumbers tease the weary bees.

Lullabies of the Garden

The flowers hum a sleepy tune,
While worms play chess beneath the moon.
A snail sings softly, oh so sweet,
While crickets tap their tiny feet.

Bumblebees wear shades so cool,
Debating which is the best school.
Ladybugs roll on the ground so round,
Inventing games that know no bound.

Colors of a Serene Solstice

In summer's glow, the colors burst,
While tomatoes joke, the peppers cursed.
A rainbow sprout lifts up its head,
Wishing for shoes instead of bread.

The carrots compete in quiet style,
Dressed in green, they stretch a mile.
With rhythm, radishes twirl and spin,
All while the cabbages wear broad grins.

Whispers from a Woven Canopy

Beneath a sky of tangled vines,
Where gossip flows through twisted twines.
A banana peel slips on the path,
Causing giggles and silly wrath.

The owls trade jokes like morning dew,
While chattering squirrels, just passing through,
Spin tales so tall they almost fly,
Underneath the giggling sky.

The Magic of Ripened Fruits

In a grove where laughter grows,
Bananas wear the silliest clothes.
Apples giggle, round and bright,
Claiming they're the star tonight.

Oranges roll with cheeky grace,
Lemons make a funny face.
Pears declare, 'We're all in sync!'
While cherries wink and tease, 'Don't blink!'

Sheltered in Nature's Grasp

Beneath a tree, a squirrel danced,
With acorns held, it pranced and pranced.
A raccoon joined, in search of snack,
Together they hatched a silly plan to unpack.

A bird chirped tunes, so off-key,
While a mouse tapped feet with glee.
Where friendship bloomed, laughter soared,
Nature's grasp, their sweet reward.

Where Shadows Dance with Light

In the twilight, shadows sway,
Mice with top hats lead the ballet.
A cat joins in, all filled with grace,
With moonbeams shining on each face.

Fireflies flicker, a disco ball,
Laughter echoes, filling the hall.
As stars peek out, the fun won't cease,
In a world where joy finds peace.

Petals of a Forgotten Tale

Once in a field, flowers conspired,
To tell a tale that never tired.
Daisies wore crowns, roses cracked jokes,
While tulips sprawled like lazy folks.

With whispers soft, secrets flew,
As bees buzzed in for a rendezvous.
Nature's chuckles filled the air,
A blooming saga beyond compare.

Wonderment in Every Bite

Each fruit giggles with delight,
Chasing bees in a sunny flight,
A pear wears spectacles so fine,
While grapes are tiptoeing the vine.

Ripe bananas dance in pairs,
While cherries trade their silly glares,
One apple claims to tell a joke,
As lemons huddle, making smoke.

With every bite, a laugh erupts,
As plums with glee do somersaults,
The harvest sings a merry song,
Beneath the sun, where fruit belongs.

Oh, what a feast of laughter here,
In silly hues, the fruits appear,
With every crunch, a chuckle springs,
And friendship's in the joy it brings.

Celestial Confections of Leaf and Branch

On leafy branches, sweets do cling,
With chocolate blooms, the birds do sing,
A whiff of cream in every breeze,
As candy frogs leap with such ease.

The caramel sun, a sticky toy,
Gives gummy squirrels their daily joy,
Peanut brittle rustles in the trees,
While licorice vines sway with the breeze.

Fizzy nectar, sparkles bright,
Flows down streams, a pure delight,
Marshmallow clouds plump and round,
Embellished by the laughter found.

Here sugar-coated dreams ignite,
In fun and frolic day and night,
Each fruit a treasure, bright and sweet,
A playground feast at nature's feet.

Vignettes of Celestial Fruits

Strawberries wear their hats of cream,
As artichokes attempt to beam,
Chortling mangos roll in cheer,
While cantaloupes just disappear.

A tangerine sings operatic tunes,
Under the watchful gaze of moons,
Pineapples gossip with ease and flair,
While kiwi fruit sparkles without a care.

Hilarity wraps round every vine,
Where fruit joins in on the fun divine,
Limes are juggling, lost in glee,
As peaches giggle, oh so free!

Each little seed a story bright,
In nature's arms, pure jovial light,
With laughter echoing through the grove,
A sweet embrace that we all love.

Petals and Secrets Caught in Light

In sunlight's warm and giggly grasp,
Petals whisper secrets, soft and fast,
The daffodils tell tales of flies,
While daisies giggle in disguise.

Laughter dances on the breeze,
As tulips tease the buzzing bees,
Each flower dons a silly hat,
And tells the sun, "Now, how 'bout that?"

Underneath the shady tree,
Mystery blooms, as wild as can be,
Lilacs waltz with the bumble bees,
In a garden full of giggling trees.

The scent of joy in every hue,
Where petals play, and laughter grew,
Caught in light, the secrets bright,
Unraveling fun—a pure delight!

Origins of Sweetness and Stardust

In a grove where fruits do giggle,
Bananas dance, and apples wiggle.
Peaches wear their fuzzy hats,
While pears are chatting with the bats.

Lemons joke about their sour fate,
Claiming they are just first-rate.
Limes reply with tangy glee,
"At least we're not stuck in a tea!"

Cherries play cards under the trees,
Catching breezes with such ease.
Grapes complain they're always squished,
While plums in pajamas dream and swished.

Sunshine laughs upon the ground,
While giggling veggies roll around.
In this patch of laughter bright,
Every day feels just right!

Where Time Stops to Bloom

In a field where daisies chat,
Butterflies wear little hats.
Time forgot its ticking game,
Flowers giggle, just the same.

Tulips gossip, trade their tips,
While bees perform their funny flips.
Roses pose in perfect rows,
While violets giggle in their clothes.

Sunsets drop their radiant rays,
As fireflies invite the plays.
The moon peeks in, takes a glance,
And joins the flowers in their dance.

Here, each hour wears a smile,
While clouds drift slowly, pause a while.
With laughter fresh, the air so sweet,
In bloom, life's a funny treat!

Treading Paths of Serenity

In a lane where shadows play,
Silly squirrels lead the way.
Bouncing branches overhead,
Tickle toes as we tread.

Winding streams hum a tune,
As ducks do their silly swoon.
Walking past the trees that yawn,
Every leaf a funny dawn.

The grass whispers quirky tales,
Of cats who sailed on paper sails.
And ants who wore their tiny crowns,
While ladies' slippers giggle down.

With every step, the world is bright,
Even the stones dance in delight.
On these paths, with every quirk,
Life's just a silly, joyful work!

The Hidden Jewel of the Vale

In a glen where secrets rest,
Magical critters are at their best.
Bunnies jump with silly cheers,
While mice juggle tiny beers.

Hidden gems of nature's art,
Laughter echoes, joy's the part.
Squirrels sneak in with their stash,
To share stories of a splash.

Clouds above wear funny hats,
While frogs croak like chatty brats.
The brook sings a giggling tune,
As daisies join the merry boon.

Here in this vale's embrace,
Life's a magic, funny place.
With every twist, a new delight,
A hidden jewel, oh what a sight!

The Dance of Sweetness

Beneath the trees, the fruits they sway,
A giggle here, a laugh's ballet.
Bananas waltz, while berries jive,
In this parade, the flavors thrive.

The apples spin in grandiose spins,
While citrus twirls, and mischief begins.
Pears toss confetti, and figs wear crowns,
Join the frolic, no room for frowns!

Lemons do the limbo, oh so low,
Cherries burst out with a vibrant glow.
With fruit as partners, let's all embrace,
A sweet tango in this zesty place!

So grab a peach, and join the fun,
In this orchard dance, we're all as one.
With laughter echoing through the land,
Grab a partner, take a fruity stand!

Chronicles of the Sun-Drenched Soil

In gardens lush, where shadows play,
The carrots joke about their stay.
Potatoes claim they're Root Kings here,
While radishes roll with raucous cheer.

The squash insists it's quite the star,
With tales of growing, wide and far.
Tomatoes blush, with laughter's glow,
As cucumbers joke about their show!

The sunflowers wink, so tall and bright,
Sharing secrets of the day and night.
Each leaf a whisper, each spore a jest,
In this sun-kissed soil, we're truly blessed.

Gather round, oh spicy greens,
Join the revelry, and see what's seen.
For in this patch of nutty delight,
The soil sings tunes from morn till night!

Secrets of the Verdant Enclave

Where the greens are lush, and laughter flies,
The broccoli plots with wide-eyed sighs.
While mushrooms giggle in their soft caps,
Joking about the plant-based mishaps.

Zucchini whispers of a squash insurrection,
But lettuce claims it's just a reflection.
With peas in pods, the stories flow,
A green tale of mischief, quite the show!

The herbs all gather for gossip divine,
Basil's in the corner, sipping thyme.
The chives chant tunes, with zest and flair,
Entertaining all, without a care.

So step inside this verdant space,
Where secrets bloom in every place.
Join the chorus, dance the green spree,
In this enclave of hilarity!

A Feast for the Imagination

With colors bright, the table is set,
A banquet of dreams, no need to fret.
Mushroom meringue and apple pie stew,
A feast that dazzles, oh, who knew?

The salad sings a harmony crisp,
While grapes giggle, just take a risk.
The punchline bubbles in a fizzy trance,
As we all gather for this dance!

Jellybeans bounce in a jelly mold,
While pickles snicker, quite bold.
With cupcakes juggling in playful jest,
It's a feast where whimsy's a welcome guest!

So let your mind take a tasty tour,
In this banquet, there's always more.
With every bite, let laughter rise,
For imagination's feast is a sweet surprise!

A Reverie in Bloom and Bounty

In a garden where laughter grows,
The carrots wear silly shoes, you know.
Tomatoes giggle, bright and round,
While the cucumbers spin round and bound.

A bee in a bowtie buzzes near,
As pumpkins sport hats without any fear.
A fruit salad jokes, it's quite a sight,
In this patch of joy, everything's bright.

Cherries with charm, they tease the pear,
Singing sweet tunes, full of happy flair.
The peppers play tag, a vibrant crew,
In a world where nonsense always feels new.

With every bloom, the fun expands,
While the radishes dance with their leafy hands.
In this cheery space, good times abound,
Where even the weeds are sillily crowned.

The Dance of Growth and Renewal

Witness sprouts in polka dots sway,
As tulips tango at the break of day.
The sunflowers sport shades, oh so bright,
While broccoli does the cha-cha in delight.

The carrots try breakdancing lows,
While peas giggle, in synchronized rows.
Spinach spins tales about old times,
As zucchini recites its rhythmic rhymes.

A ladybug leads the grand parade,
With fireflies lighting up the cascade.
A party unfolds beneath the trees,
With umbrella mushrooms swaying in the breeze.

In this fest of growth, joy is alive,
As cacti do the twist, trying to thrive.
With every seed, laughter does bloom,
In the waltz of nature, there's always room.

A Garden's Heartbeat

Under the soil, a ticklish root,
Pops a potato in polka-dot suit.
With every beat, the garden sings,
As beet greens jiggle, sprouting springs.

Sun-kissed sprouts do the shake and sway,
As butterflies join the fun display.
Radishes giggle in colors so bright,
While eggplant wears shades, what a sight!

In the midst of each leafy call,
A prancing pea plant makes us all fall.
With laughter echoing through the green,
Even the dirt feels the joy unseen.

Amidst the chaos, seeds find their way,
In a carnival dance, they twirl and play.
With every heartbeat, nature's tune flows,
Creating a tapestry where silliness grows.

Luminous Nights in the Grove

Fireflies dance in the air,
Shadows giggle everywhere.
Raccoons play cards by the tree,
While owls hoot in glee.

Cherries burst with a pop!
While bear suits make everyone stop.
Lost socks float in the breeze,
As squirrels wear hats with ease.

The moon's a giant disco ball,
Reflecting laughter over all.
Fruits gossip, oh what a sight,
Holding a party deep in the night.

Lemons jive with melons in line,
Bananas breakdance, oh so fine.
In this grove of silly delight,
Nature's humor shines ever bright.

The Realm of Infinite Harvest

Peas in pods sing a tune,
While vegetables race to the moon.
Pumpkins polish their orange hue,
In a game of peek-a-boo!

Cabbages play hide and seek,
While silly radishes squeak.
Corn on the cob wears a crown,
As carrots parade through town.

Bees wear tiny, buzzing hats,
Chasing away the sleepy cats.
Pineapples stuck in a tree,
Yell, 'Come share this juicy spree!'

Underneath the leafy roof,
Laughter echoes, that's the proof.
In this realm where harvests thrive,
Every silly joke's alive.

Fruition of Forgotten Tales

Old apples spin stories unfit,
While grapes giggle, a sweet little bit.
Oranges get lost in their joy,
As peaches play with a toy!

Lemons tell tales of sour glee,
While apricots sip on sweet tea.
Cherries paint the sky with dreams,
In this land where laughter beams.

Kiwi kittens cuddle so tight,
As berries kindle their spark in the night.
Figs throw a ball, catch some fun,
While everyone dances, everyone runs!

With each bite, the tales unfold,
A banquet of laughter, bravely bold.
In the orchard, where whims unite,
Beneath the stars, everything's bright.

Transience in a Sea of Green

Lettuce rode on a tiny wave,
While radishes dance, feeling brave.
Spinach sings a soft goodbye,
As cabbages reach for the sky.

Beets play tricks until the dusk,
While broccoli smells of musk.
A garden chair made of vines,
Hosts tomatoes that sip on wines.

Inquisitive peas peek from the leaves,
Telling tales that truly deceives.
Zucchini debates with a squirrel,
As flowers twirl and swirl.

Seasons chuckle as they pass,
Each moment caught in dappled grass.
In this patch where laughter's flees,
Time's a funny breeze through the trees.

Echoes of the Abundant Land

In a field where laughter hides,
Giant carrots dance with pride.
Pickles play a game of tag,
While tomatoes wear a silly rag.

Bees in bow ties buzz around,
Chasing shadows on the ground.
Mice with hats sip lemonade,
As squirrels in suits are unafraid.

A cabbage king takes his throne,
With a crown of thyme, all his own.
The corn stalks whisper tales of cheer,
Of a pie-eating contest near!

Lemonade rivers flow with glee,
And jellybean trees sway carefree.
In this land of quirky fun,
Every day's a race to run.

Mysteries Among the Petals

In a garden where jokes take flight,
Sunflowers wink in the morning light.
Roses giggle, blushing bright,
As daisies dance, oh what a sight!

Beetles croon their latest hit,
While butterflies do a funny skit.
Insects wear their finest threads,
For the grand ball beneath their beds.

Tulips tease with colors bold,
Whispers of stories yet untold.
A bee wears glasses, ponders deep,
While ladybugs begin to leap.

Mysteries bloom in vibrant hues,
Where laughter brews with fragrant views.
Join the fun, don't miss the cue,
In this garden of whimsical dew!

A Tapestry of Tasty Dreams

In a market where flavors collide,
A pickle pie makes giggles slide.
Chocolate rivers swirl around,
As dancing donuts bounce and bound.

Gummy bears play hide and seek,
While jellybeans start to speak.
Marshmallow clouds float on high,
With popcorn kernels twirling by.

Peaches wear a crown of cream,
In this land of tasty dreams.
Watermelon bands play funky tunes,
Underneath the disco moons.

Syrup falls like sweet rain drops,
While candy canes do funny hops.
In this world of sugary schemes,
Giggles rise in tasty streams!

Shadows of the Sunlit Glade

In the glade where shadows tease,
Wiggly worms wear tiny skis.
Bunnies juggle carrots bright,
Underneath the dappled light.

A juggling fox, a foxy act,
Flops and flips, then fades to black.
Frogs with flutes croon a silly song,
As giggling critters join along.

Sunbeams dance between the trees,
Tickling leaves in a gentle breeze.
While acorns roll with glee anew,
In a nutty game of peekaboo.

Under the shadowy sway so light,
Chasing dreams takes joyous flight.
In this glade of playful grace,
Healthiest laughter finds its place!

Reflections on a Fruitful Journey

In a land where apples gleam,
A squirrel stole a real big dream.
He grabbed the pie and took a bite,
Then ran away with quite a fright.

The pears were laughing in the trees,
While berries danced upon the breeze.
They tickled noses passing by,
As giggles filled the sunny sky.

A peach once wore a silly hat,
Declared himself the biggest brat.
The plums just rolled their eyes so wide,
While cherries laughed and tried to hide.

With every fruit and every cheer,
A journey filled with laughter here.
Who knew a grove could spark such glee?
A fruity world of jubilee!

Savoring Nature's Bounty

A banana slipped and fell with grace,
It skidded right into a case.
The lemons rolled, oh what a sight,
A citrus dance in morning light.

Grapes in clusters started prancing,
While oranges began romancing.
They squeezed each other, laughter loud,
As fruits formed up a jolly crowd.

Kiwi tried to tell a tale,
But tangled up within its peel.
The laugh that burst cracked open smiles,
As fruits united across the miles.

When nature gives a bountiful treat,
You find it's hard to stay off beat.
So let the laughter fill your soul,
In every bite, there's joy, a goal!

Blushing Blossoms and Moonlit Nights

Beneath the moon, the fruits all blushed,
With giggles soft, they quickly rushed.
A tomato danced with merry flair,
And radishes combed their frizzy hair.

The apples whispered midnight dreams,
While pears made wishes with their beams.
They played until the sun would rise,
With jests that sparked the sleepy skies.

At twilight's call, the peaches twirled,
In blossoms bright, their joys unfurled.
They shared a pie that burst with cheer,
As fireflies joined, the night drew near.

Amidst the fun, they laughed and played,
In moonlit warmth, they were not swayed.
For in this grove, the magic's clear,
Each quiet moment loud with cheer!

Enchanted Rustlings of the Grove

In the grove, a rumor spread,
That carrots wore their tops like red.
The leafy greens all whispered sly,
As fruits just shook their heads and cried.

Pineapples vied for tallest crown,
While zucchinis danced all around.
The playful vines, with mischief rife,
Plotted to steal the veggie life.

A fruit fly flew, all full of pride,
Claiming it was the wittiest guide.
But static cling from peachy fuzz,
Caught it in laughter, it was a buzz.

They gathered close for one last jest,
Together they would be the best.
In rustling leaves and playful tone,
An enchanted grove where joy is grown.

Echoing Laughter of the Foliage

In the trees, jokes are ripe,
Apples giggle, never type.
Bananas slip on silly tales,
Dancing squirrels, one winks, one pales.

Lemons squirt with witty puns,
While cherries race for golden runs.
Bouncing leaves, they clap and cheer,
A fruit parade, oh what a sphere!

Plums tell tales of blushing days,
As pears perform in laugh-filled plays.
Every branch a giggle jumps,
Underneath, the ground just humps.

So wander through this merry grove,
Where laughter lives, and antics rove.
In every nook, find joy anew,
The foliage grins, it's all for you.

Scented Whispers in the Breeze

Whispers float on scented air,
Peaches blush with fragrant flair.
Jasmine giggles, smells like fun,
While nuts play hide and seek in sun.

Minty leaves, they tease and jest,
Tickling noses, it's the best.
Breezes carry chuckles sweet,
As daisies dance on sprightly feet.

Raspberry whispers, soft and sly,
Invite you in with a winked eye.
Grapes roll by like merry thieves,
In a game that laughs and weaves.

Cotton candy clouds above,
As nature's heart beats, full of love.
Here the silly scents tickle your mind,
In a breeze where joys unwind.

Mirages Amidst the Green

Mirages swirl in leafy sight,
Where fruits play tricks in morning light.
Cucumbers clown in sunlit spree,
While peppers jiggle, wild and free.

Lettuce lays down, takes a nap,
Sandwich dreams, oh what a trap!
Tomatoes burst with laughter bright,
A salad party, pure delight.

Avocados roll, a comic show,
Mangoes wink; it's quite the row.
While every sprout begins to grin,
The garden hums—a laugh within.

So weave through greens, take a peek,
In nature's laugh, we find our cheek.
Amidst the mirages, joy we seek,
For in the green, the funny speaks.

Treading on Dreams of Juicy Past

Walking soft on squishy ground,
Banana peels make quite the sound.
Grapefruit giggles as you pass,
Its zesty laugh—a fruity brass.

Berry bushes whisper tales,
Of dreams that dance and jest like sails.
Cotton candy clouds droop low,
As cherry blossoms steal the show.

Mirthful roots tickle your toes,
Underfoot, where laughter grows.
Pastel shades of fruit-filled cheer,
Echo loudly for all to hear.

So tread on dreams where laughter sows,
Juicy tales in every rose.
In this realm of whimsy cast,
You'll find delight from sorrows past.

Whispers of the Gnarled Trees

In the shade of the twisted trunk,
A squirrel sings, a joyful junk.
The branches sway, a silly dance,
Beneath the leaves, the critters prance.

A raccoon with a bandit's eye,
Steals apples as they roll and fly.
The old tree chuckles, creaks with glee,
While bees buzz softly, 'Oh, woe is me!'

The wind joins in with a playful call,
As acorns tumble, ready to fall.
Each fruit a gem of laughter bright,
In this green realm of pure delight.

So sit beneath, let worries cease,
Join the frolic, enjoy the peace.
In these gnarled boughs, where fun is free,
Find joy in nature's whimsy spree.

Enchanted Harvest

Pickles grown on vines so tall,
Unruly cucumbers winging a brawl.
With every step, they wiggle and squeak,
A veggie patch that's gone quite unique.

The tomatoes blush with every tease,
Chatting with beans in the gentle breeze.
Radishes play hide and seek,
While pumpkins giggle, 'Aren't we chic?'

Harvest time, such playful cheer,
Carrots bouncing, "Come grab a beer!"
The cornfields whisper silly jokes,
As joyful laughter fills the oaks.

In every row, a surprise awaits,
With chortling herbs and dancing plates.
Each bite a burst of happiness found,
In this magical garden underground.

Fruits of the Forgotten

Once hid the bananas, lost and shy,
They giggle now as they tumble by.
The pears congregate, a moody bunch,
Hiding from the apples after lunch.

An old grape vine starts to sway,
"Join the party, don't delay!"
Licorice twists with a cheeky grin,
While cherries bounce, let the feast begin!

Each fruit recalls a tale of yore,
Of silly sprites and playful lore.
The rascal fruitcake stirs the mix,
"Mischief's the game, now watch the tricks!"

So take a bite, and hold on tight,
For in this patch, whimsy takes flight.
With colors bright, and laughter to lend,
These forgotten fruits are the best of friends.

Colorful Tales from the Canopy

High above, the colors burst,
In leafy laughter, chatter, and thirst.
The parrots sing in a cheeky band,
Each swing they take is perfectly planned.

Vines twist like snakes in a silly race,
While a chameleon finds its place.
Fruit bats giggle, sipping the sweet,
As sunbeams dance on the mossy seat.

In the embrace of the leafy crown,
Nature spins tales of a wiggly clown.
A chubby owl hoots a joke so sly,
While the eagles soar, oh so high!

So let's gather round in this bright bazaar,
Where stories echo, near and far.
In the colors bright, let fun be key,
In the canopy's heart, we'll find pure glee.

Echoing Laughter Amongst the Boughs

A squirrel spins tales, so grand,
While birds gossip, plucking at strands.
The apples chuckle, round and red,
Whispering secrets, laughter widespread.

Beneath the trees, a fox prances,
Joining in on the merry dances.
With every bounce, a silly sound,
Echoing joy all around the ground.

Bees buzz like they're telling a joke,
While rabbits giggle, hearts bespoke.
A cat, with a grin, claims a throne,
In this cheerful kingdom, all laugh alone.

The sun beams down, a playful glare,
Filling the air with warmth to share.
In every corner, a chuckle thrives,
The humor here is what truly survives.

A Journey Through Nature's Palette

With colors bright, the path is clear,
As daisies waltz, smiling ear to ear.
The oranges blush, the greens do sway,
Nature's jesters, in a lively play.

A purple grape slips with a cheer,
Rolling downhill, oh dear, oh dear!
While butterflies joke, in flight so free,
With their painted wings, in bright jubilee.

The sunflowers nod, with heads held high,
Counting the clouds as they pass by.
Each shade a laugh, each hue a jest,
In this canvas of mirth, we're truly blessed.

A rainbow arcs, with shades galore,
Making us giggle, and then some more.
Nature's laughter colors the scene,
In this vibrant world, all is serene.

Caressed by Gentle Breezes

The wind whispers jokes as it breezes by,
Tickling the branches, oh me, oh my!
Leaves dance along in a spinning spree,
Nature's own laughter, wild and free.

A dandelion bursts, sending seeds away,
Like fluffy parachutes, in a playful display.
Each gust a chuckle, a whimsical tease,
Bringing forth giggles, as light as air leaves.

Clouds shape like animals, soft and round,
Chasing each other, never quite found.
With each puff of air, the laughter ascends,
Playing on lips, just like close friends.

Under the skies, we frolic and soar,
In breezy whispers, we're wanting more.
All around us, the fun never ceases,
A jolly world, where joy increases.

The Language of Rustling Leaves

The leaves have secrets, swirling around,
Whispering tales in a rustling sound.
One tells of acorns, shy and neat,
While others debate who's tasting the beet.

A child runs past, and they all sway,
Joining the giggles in a leafy ballet.
The twigs snap like laughter, crisp and clear,
Adding to the chorus, let's all adhere.

In the branches above, the breezes conspire,
Tickling the leaves like they're on a wire.
Each giggle translates through sunlight's weave,
The signs of merriment, hard to believe.

So, pause for a moment, lend an ear,
To the playful leaves, calling you near.
In their rustling language, there's humor untold,
Stories of fun, in nature enfold.

Blooms That Tell Stories

In the garden, laughter grows,
Petals whisper, secrets flow.
A sunflower sways, wearing shades,
Joking with bees, their dance parades.

Roses giggle with a poke,
Thorns tease and make a joke.
Tulips in tuxedos, what a sight,
Hosting parties every night.

Daffodils drop punchlines bright,
While daisies bask in morning light.
Nature's jesters, bold and spry,
Blooming tales as clouds drift by.

The Arcane Allure of Green

Mossy stones with a knowing grin,
Whispering tales of where they've been.
Frogs in hats, they croak with flair,
Imagining themselves as debonair.

Sassy snails in a race so sly,
Moving slow but aiming high.
Vines that twirl like dancers at night,
Pulling pranks with all their might.

Lettuce wraps with a witty shout,
Leafy greens just love to sprout.
In emerald realms, the fun won't cease,
Where every frond finds sweet release.

Golden Hours in the Garden

Sunsets stretch with a warm embrace,
Bouncing bumblebees full of grace.
Chasing shadows, they twist and twirl,
While dandelions decide to hurl.

Grasshoppers play the trombone loud,
Gathering nature's silly crowd.
Twilight croaks from a frog's fair laugh,
As fireflies join the evening's path.

The sunbeams wink from leafy heights,
Inviting giggles into the nights.
Cucumbers in capes wave goodbye,
As the moon comes up to say hi.

Fables Beneath Glorious Canopies

Underneath the leafy dome,
Animals gather, far from home.
A squirrel tells tales of wild delight,
Of acorns snatched in the dead of night.

Owls share wisdom with a wink,
While bats just flap and start to stink.
Tales of mischief, laughter sprees,
Spin around the ancient trees.

The canopy laughs with a rustling song,
Where every critter feels they belong.
In this realm of mischief so grand,
Fables unfold with a playful hand.

Beneath the Gnarled Branches

Beneath the gnarled branches, the squirrels play,
They dance with the shadows, in a nutty ballet.
A raccoon wears glasses, with a book in his hand,
Reading tales of the woods, isn't it quite grand?

The apples are giggling, the pears start to tease,
The lemons are plotting, they aim to appease.
A frog in a top hat hops by with a grin,
"Who knew fruits could joke? Let the fun now begin!"

A worm in a bowtie gives speeches profound,
On the art of fine chewing, his wisdom renowned.
The rows of bright berries cheer with delight,
As the fruit party rages throughout the night!

So come to this haven, where laughter's the creed,
Join friends who are fruity, in a world full of speed.
With each twist and turn, there's magic and cheer,
Beneath the gnarled branches, adventure is near!

Hidden Treasures of the Grove

In a place where the sunbeams bring shadows to cheer,
Hidden treasures are buried, or so says the deer.
With maps made of leaves and the scent of the breeze,
They hunt for the secrets among the tall trees.

A snail in a treasure chest, proudly displayed,
Claiming his riches are worth a parade!
The mushrooms are giggling, all spots in a row,
As whispers of secrets begin to grow.

A hedgehog's domain is where pranks often land,
He sharpens his quills, his defenses all planned.
With acorns for cannonballs and laughter that rings,
They joyfully pounce, oh the fun that it brings!

As evening draws near, with a wink and a nod,
The treasures await; so come join the squad.
For where fun is the goal, and friends make it sweet,
Hidden joys of the grove can't be beat!

Serendipity Amongst the Leaves

Amongst the leaves where the giggles abound,
Serendipity bounces and rolls on the ground.
A butterfly whispers a secret or two,
That apples once danced with bananas; it's true!

The cucumbers chuckle, "Let's play hide and seek!"
They peek from their patches, so bold and so cheek.
While onions all cry, but just out of joy,
As they watch the fun filled with laughter, oh boy!

A pear slips and tumbles, then laughs on the way,
"Who knew that this grove could be such a play?"
And just when you think that the fun is all done,
A tomato does a cartwheel, oh what a run!

So come join the party, let silliness reign,
Where every lost seed can blossom again.
With joy in the air and surprises to weave,
It's pure serendipity amidst the green leaves!

Sunlit Dreams of Harvest

In morning's embrace, where sunflowers grin,
The dreams of the harvest are beginning to spin.
A pumpkin wearing shades struts down the lane,
While radishes giggle, all dressed up in rain.

Cucumbers boast of their long, funny shape,
While broccoli plots to escape from the drape.
Each berry declares it's the juiciest prize,
While carrots in costumes parade 'neath blue skies.

A scarecrow with socks that are mismatched and bright,
Sways dance steps with glee through the soft golden light.
As bees buzz tunes that they hum with great flair,
The sunlit dreams twirl in the harvest affair!

So come to the fields where laughter's the rule,
With smiles wrapped in sunshine, oh what a cool duel!
In dreams of tomorrow, with joy we will bask,
For the harvest of laughter is our only task!

The Ethereal Glow of Growth

In a garden where giggles grow,
Sunflowers wear hats, don't you know?
Worms parade in tuxedos bold,
Roots whisper secrets, tales untold.

Bees in bowties buzz with flair,
Tickling petals, without a care.
Frogs in the shade hold a grand soiree,
Sipping dew like it's cabernet!

Trees tell jokes that make you pine,
Ripe apples cheer, "We're truly divine!"
Even the grass gets in on the fun,
Doing cartwheels under the sun.

As night falls, the veggies glow bright,
Carrots in pajamas, what a sight!
With laughter echoing through the night,
This garden's magic feels just right.

Dance of the Gentle Rain

Drops tap-danced on the roof with glee,
While puddles giggled—"Come jump with me!"
Raindrops played a merry tune,
While clouds wore smiles, bright as the moon.

Squirrels twirled in tiny boots,
Dancing like they'd found their roots.
Each blade of grass did a shimmy-shake,
While ducks quacked jokes, just for the lake.

Grasshoppers leapt with a silly sway,
As frogs crooned songs to lead the way.
The rain spun tales that made it rain,
With every drop, more smiles gained.

When the downpour finally ceased,
A rainbow formed, the colors increased!
Nature's revelry, a grand parade,
Bright laughter lingers in the glade.

Fruitful Whispers

Strawberries giggle in their red attire,
While blueberries dance, a fruity choir.
Bananas declare they're the top of the bunch,
Joking about peaches who just love to munch.

Oranges tumble, roll with flair,
Squeezing puns, they hang in the air.
The grapes gossip, they're quite the bunch,
Sharing tales as they share a lunch.

Pineapples wear crowns, feeling regal and fine,
Wishing they could join the grapevine.
Every flavor whispers, secrets so sweet,
In this fruitful haven, laughter's the treat.

Even the lemons, sour yet bright,
Crack the best jokes, a true delight!
In this garden where humor is ripe,
The fruit flies high, there's always a type!

Boughs of Enchantment

Under trees with character and grace,
Squirrels hold court in a leafy place.
Branches croon as the wind gives a shove,
While bugs in tuxedos dance with love.

Acorns play drums on a squirrel's request,
As butterflies flutter, they look their best.
The birch bark whispers secrets and lies,
While owls hoot tales 'neath magical skies.

Each branch sways lightly, like a gentle bow,
As shadows waltz on the soft mossy plough.
Peacocks tease with feathers so bright,
Joking they're stars of the night's vibrant light.

With each rustle, laughter merges with breeze,
In this enchanted bough, hearts feel at ease.
Magic awaits, as the branches embrace,
A hilarity realm, a whimsical place.

Fruits of Whimsy

In a land where bananas wear hats,
And apples dance with friendly bats,
Cherries giggle, hanging low,
While silly pears put on a show.

Lemons slide on a peel so bright,
Oranges juggle, oh what a sight!
Raspberries burst with laughter loud,
As grapes gather 'round, feeling proud.

Kiwis whisper jokes so sweet,
While pineapples tap their tiny feet,
Mangoes spin in a fruity ballet,
Oh, what fun in this fruity fray!

In this garden, joy won't cease,
Where every fruit offers some peace,
With whimsies ripe upon each tree,
A jester's hat is the best to see!

Blossoms of Daring Days

On daring days when the sun is bold,
A coconut tells tales of old,
While tulips wear their brightest shades,
And daisies plot their fun crusades.

Roses don their best disguises,
To masquerade as sweet surprises,
Violets giggle, poking fun,
At bumblebees who just can't run.

Sunflowers do the cha-cha slide,
As butterflies take their wild ride,
Petunias whisper, 'Let's take a chance,'
Under skies that sparkle and dance.

With every bloom, a chuckle grows,
In lands where cheeky mischief flows,
Daring days bring laughter's sway,
Flowers frolic in bright display!

Secrets Hidden Beneath the Boughs

Beneath the branches, secrets lie,
A plum in glasses, oh my, oh my!
A wise old walnut guards the ground,
While sneaky squirrels just dart around.

Peaches ponder, 'What to do?'
'Should we dance or have a stew?'
Fig trees chuckle, sharing tales,
Of nuts that dream of epic trails.

Hidden treasures, whispers low,
In shadows where mischief loves to grow,
Grapevines giggle, tangled tight,
Unraveling secrets, day and night.

With every breeze, a giggle stirs,
While garden gnomes exchange purrs,
Beneath the boughs so thick and deep,
Laughter lingers, never sleeps!

Dreamscapes in a Grove

In a grove where dreams take flight,
A melon twirls in moonlit light,
With citrus fables all around,
While dreaming fruits tumble down.

Bananas wearing tiny capes,
Plotting journeys to silly shapes,
Avocados float on clouds of cream,
In this whimsical, fruity dream.

Lime fairies dance on rainbow paths,
Drawing chalk with leafy wraths,
Their laughter echoes through the leaves,
As everyone dreams of joyful eves.

In this grove where giggles soar,
Fruity fantasies forevermore,
Each dreamer's wish takes colorful form,
In a place where whimsy is the norm!

Secrets of the Ripened Bough

In the branches, secrets hide,
With squirrels wearing hats with pride.
Each fruit holds a tale, quite absurd,
A pie-fight promised with just a word.

Dancing bees in bowler hats,
They buzz and giggle, oh what slats!
A moonlit feast with lemonade,
Who knew such fun could be displayed?

Peaches call, 'Come and take a nibble!'
While apricots chuckle, 'Just a dribble!'
The plums wink back, a cheeky crew,
A raucous riot, who knew they'd brew?

Underneath the leafy shroud,
Nature's laughter sings out loud.
With every swing of mischief's bow,
Secrets bloom on the ripened bough.

Whimsy Among the Petals

In a garden where giggles grow,
Flowers boast in a vibrant show.
They wear polka dots, stripes, and lace,
Each petal dances, a joyful grace.

Butterflies flutter on sticks and dots,
Telling puns that tie up knots.
'What did the rose say to the bee?'
'Buzz off, buddy, can't you see?'

Tulips joke as they wave their heads,
'Watch your step, or you'll wake the reds!'
Daisies chuckle in the sun's soft light,
Holding a comedy show every night.

With laughter echoing all around,
The petals giggle, joy unbound.
In this whimsical, flowery spree,
Nature plays its jester, so carefree.

A Dance of Light and Fruit

Under stars with fruits so bright,
Bananas schedule a silly fight.
'That apple thinks he's such a star!'
'Just wait,' says lemon, 'I'll raise the bar!'

Grapes gather in a jubilant train,
Rolling down the lane—oh, what a gain!
They tickle the oranges with a wink,
Together, they make the best drink.

Cherries dance in a lively whip,
Twirling like they're on a rocket ship.
Kiwi and mango join the fun,
While passion fruits bask in the sun.

The night hums with giggles and cheers,
Nature's banquet, nothing but peers.
Join the revels, let laughter suit,
In this dance of light and fruit!

The Veil of Nature's Canvas

With splashes of color and giggles galore,
Nature paints jokes on every shore.
In this canvas, the sun's a clown,
Brushing the hills with a golden gown.

Clouds wear hats of marshmallow fluff,
While raindrops tap out a tune that's rough.
The flowers laugh and join the spree,
They tic-tac-toe on the grass so free.

Bees play drums with their buzzing sound,
While frogs croak rhythmically all around.
Oh what a ruckus, a cheerful sight,
Nature's canvas, painted bright!

So raise your cup to the merry spree,
To colors and laughter, wild and free.
Underneath this veil, don't be shy—
Join the jests of the earth and sky!

The Breeze that Carries Secrets

Upon the breeze, whispers float,
Telling tales of a sneaky goat.
He wears a hat, two sizes too wide,
And prances around with questionable pride.

In this land of giggles and glee,
The trees share gossip, just you and me.
If you look closely, you might find,
A squirrel laughing, oh so unkind!

Nuts are traded for riddles galore,
While the flowers roll on the forest floor.
A butterfly flutters, with mischief in tow,
As the breeze lifts secrets, ready to go.

The grass tickles toes in a playful jest,
While the sun grins down, feeling so blessed.
Join the laughter, don't be shy,
For in this wonder, we all can fly!

Mirth in a Tangle of Vines

In the vines, where shadows twist,
A farmer swears he's made a list.
Of all the vegetables, ripe and round,
But forgot the carrots, oh how profound!

Tomatoes giggle, peas join the fun,
As pumpkins roll, oh, they can run!
The scarecrow's hat is blown away,
As cackling birds steal the day.

The cucumber juggles, what a delight,
While onions cry, not out of fright.
A dance ensues, roots tapping in time,
To the rhythm of laughter, oh so sublime.

So if you wander through the green,
Watch out for silliness, never serene.
In a tangle, where mirth finds its way,
Join in the laughter, come what may!

Beyond the Rustling Leaves

Beyond the leaves, a ruckus brews,
As raccoons play dress-up, in mismatched shoes.
They strut and pose, with pride in their eyes,
While a lowly frog judges their size.

In the underbrush, foxes proclaim,
That hide-and-seek is their favorite game.
One plays the seeker, with a tail so sly,
While the others just snicker as they hide nearby.

A crow caws loudly, with a jest in mind,
Spreading rumors of a turtle who's blind.
Yet that turtle, wise beyond his years,
Knows exactly where he is, despite the jeers.

So wander forth, and lend an ear,
To whispers of laughter, loud and clear.
For in the rustling, where fun is free,
Adventure awaits, come find the key!

A Symphony of Scented Blooms

In a garden lush, where flowers play,
The daisies giggle, swaying all day.
A daffodil dances, twirling around,
While the bees buzz sweetly, a merry sound.

The lavender laughs, with a fragrance divine,
As tulips tease, and the roses align.
A gentle wind carries their voice,
Making the bees buzz and the frogs rejoice.

Sunflowers stand tall, with heads held high,
Saying, "Join us, dear friends, let's all comply!"
But the peonies pout, not fully aware,
That their perfume brings joy, floating in air.

Amidst the petals, where scents unite,
A symphony blooms, pure delight.
So stop for a moment, soak up the cheer,
Join the floral frolic, let's all draw near!

Secrets Beneath the Canopy

Beneath the leaves, a squirrel hides,
Whispers of gossip on sunshine rides.
A puppet show among the roots,
Where ants wear hats and dance in boots.

Chipmunks gossip, with tales so grand,
About a garden gnome who can't stand.
They spill their secrets, one by one,
While ladybugs giggle under the sun.

The breeze carries tales of veggies bold,
A cabbage crowned with a crown of gold.
Moos from a cow who thinks she's a horse,
And carrots that plot a daring course.

In shadows, mischief is always afoot,
A rogue tomato, wearing a boot.
With every rustle, laughter ignites,
In this playful world, full of delights.

Blossoms in the Moonlight

At night, the blossoms wear silly hats,
With petals that dance like playful cats.
Bees in tuxedos, sipping sweet tea,
Join in the frolic, wild and free.

Moonlit nights, a perfect time,
For flowers to giggle, in rhythm and rhyme.
A tulip sneezes, oh what a fright!
Sending its cousins into a flight.

The lilies start telling knock-knock jokes,
While crickets laugh and tumble like folks.
A daffodil trips, all covered in dew,
Saying, "Watch out, I'm coming for you!"

In this garden where silliness blooms,
Even the owls are cracking cartoons.
Under the stars, laughter takes flight,
In the glow of the cosmos, everyone's bright.

A Tapestry of Flora

A patchwork quilt of greens and gold,
Adventures in leaves, waiting to unfold.
Sunflowers wear shades, striking a pose,
While violets giggle, tickling their toes.

The daisies play tag, with bees in the lead,
Over hills, they scamper and speed.
A garden gnome trips, the poor little lad,
Shouting, "Watch out! This isn't so rad!"

Mushrooms debate on who looks the best,
With polka dots that steal the fest.
Every bloom boasts of tales from afar,
Like marigolds swaying, "We're all a star!"

Nature's stage set, with a whimsical flare,
Where cacti sing songs, quite beyond compare.
In this world, where laughter can grow,
The joy of the flora is all in the show.

Echoes of Autumn's Embrace

Autumn arrives with a jolly cheer,
Squirrels throw acorns, don't you dare near!
Leaves doing ballet, twirling through air,
While pumpkins giggle, beyond compare.

The wind's a comedian, tickling the trees,
With whispers of jest in the crispy breeze.
Apples play hide and seek in the grass,
"Did you find me? Oops, here comes a pass!"

The colors collide in a playful spree,
As critters in costumes flap by with glee.
A mischievous crow with a cape and a mask,
"Catch me if you can!" is his daring task.

In this season where laughter does peek,
Nature's own laughter is around every creek.
With every rustle and chuckle so bright,
Autumn's embrace is pure delight.

Twilight's Gentle Caress

In the hush of twilight's glow,
Silly critters start to show,
A raccoon dons a silly hat,
And dances with a chubby cat.

The fireflies begin to twirl,
As frogs leap and give a whirl,
A squirrel juggles acorns high,
While night winds whisper soft and shy.

Laughter echoes through the trees,
As bumblebees hum melodies,
A parrot starts to sing a tune,
That makes the owls laugh and swoon.

In this place, where smiles abound,
Each day brings joy that knows no bound,
With funny games and silly pranks,
Nature's humor fills the ranks.

The Melody of Swaying Limbs

Beneath the branches, laughter rings,
As swing sets made of two old springs,
Are occupied by goats in masks,
While trees perform their funny tasks.

A parrot tells a corny joke,
While playful raccoons steal a cloak,
The wind begins a tickly dance,
As flowers giggle, and they prance.

A bear attempts to do a jig,
While frogs cheer on, each step so big,
A chorus sings from high above,
To keep the spirit full of love.

In this realm of great delight,
Where everything seems just so right,
Each sunset brings a silly cheer,
For nature's jesters draw us near.

Beneath the Canopy of Stars

Underneath a twinkling dome,
Silly owls paint a funny poem,
As stars waltz for the moonlit stage,
And giggly fairies free their rage.

The crickets tune their tiny strings,
As playful fireflies flap their wings,
A constellational game is played,
With cosmic laughter arrayed.

A hedgehog sings a lullaby,
While raccoons try to grasp the sky,
In this spot where dreams take flight,
Giggles echo, pure delight.

As morning breaks, the laughter fades,
Yet whispers rest in secret glades,
For every night brings tales anew,
Just waiting for a laugh or two.

A Cornucopia of Wonder

In a garden full of playful sights,
Where veggies wear their finest tights,
A tomato rolls down the hill,
While carrots giggle, what a thrill!

Potatoes dance in twinkling shoes,
While radishes sing the latest blues,
A cabbage tries its hand at mime,
As nature shares its jester's rhyme.

With each turn, surprise evolves,
As pumpkins plot their funny solves,
A cornfield sways to banter bright,
Creating joy from morning light.

So gather 'round this playful scene,
Where laughter reigns and hearts are keen,
In this world of sweet delight,
Every moment laughs goodnight.

Abundance Under the Sun's Gaze

Fruit hangs low with a cheeky grin,
Lemons dance, and apples spin.
Bouncing berries wave hello,
While pumpkins play in the show.

Peaches giggle, their cheeks so round,
In between laughs, they tumble down.
Grapes in hats sharing a jest,
Nature's humor at its best.

Cherries throw a party loud,
Inviting everyone in the crowd.
Bananas slip on their own peel,
Joyous chaos, oh what a meal!

Under the sun, it's quite a sight,
Every fruit is a comedian bright.
With laughter sprouting from every vine,
It's a fruity carnival, purely divine!

Nature's Palette Paints Serenity

Colors explode like confetti bright,
Each hue giggles in sheer delight.
The daisies twirl in sunny glee,
While roses wink, 'Come dance with me!'

Bluebells jive without a care,
While violets trade their tales rare.
Lemons dressed in zesty zest,
Join the flowers, feeling blessed.

Sunflowers beam, their heads held high,
Winking at clouds that pass by.
Petunias chuckle, painting the air,
With colors and laughter everywhere.

A canvas of joy, mirth unrivaled,
Nature's brush, whimsically wild.
With every petal, a secret's unfurled,
In this playground, laughter's twirled!

The Soliloquy of Ripened Fruits

A watermelon sighs with juicy dreams,
Ripe with whispers, or so it seems.
Peaches blush with a wink and a grin,
While cherries chat about where to begin.

Bananas boast of their slip-and-slide,
While mangoes giggle, oh what a ride!
Oranges chirp with zest so grand,
Debating who's the best in this land.

Pineapples argue over who is prickly,
But in the end, all are quite tricky.
With puns and laughs in a fruity show,
Each verse a laugh, watch friendships grow.

In their soliloquy, wisdom's shared,
Sharing secrets, none are spared.
Each fruit a character, vibrant and bright,
Crafting tales of hilarious plight!

Journeying Among Nature's Gifts

Take a stroll through vineyards of cheer,
With grapes that giggle, so sincere.
Pumpkins roll on their plump little feet,
While carrots compete in their dance so sweet.

Berries form a parade in the sun,
Laughing and joking, just having fun.
Cucumbers wear their best green suits,
Swinging and swaying, oh what a hoot!

Tomatoes throw a salsa groove,
With basil joining in the move.
Fields of veggies, lively and spry,
Under the big blue, they reach for the sky.

As the sun sets, the fruits whisper tales,
In their land of laughter, where joy never fails.
Journeying here, where giggles abound,
In the dance of the gifts that nature's found!

Leafy Sanctuaries of Bliss

In a garden so green, the squirrels do dance,
Chasing their tails, they leap and prance.
With acorns as hats, they party in style,
While cheeky green frogs croak, 'Just stay for a while!'

Bumblebees buzz with a comical hum,
Accidentally mistaking folks for their chum.
They land on a nose, then zoom up like jets,
Wishing for honey, not BBQ sets!

A snail wears a shell that's too big for his back,
Dreaming of rocket rides down the dirt track.
'Faster!' he shouts, 'I'm late for my date!'
With a ladybug waiting, it's sure to be great!

In this leafy escape, laughter takes flight,
Where mischief and merriment shine ever bright.
So join in the fun, with the critters bizarre,
For happiness blooms, wherever you are!

Rhythms of Sun and Soil

The sun's a comedian on its daily stage,
Tickling the flowers, igniting their rage.
'Why do daisies look surprised every day?'
'Because every time, they just can't run away!'

Worms wiggle and giggle, they're digging for gold,
While butterflies dance, their stories unfold.
They flutter in circles, a comic ballet,
'Got any jokes?' they inquire with a sway!

Oh, the radishes shout, 'We're rooting for fun!'
While tomatoes blush bright, they bask in the sun.
With laughter and chatter, the garden's alive,
This patch of pure joy makes everyone thrive!

In rhythms of soil, the laughter is grand,
Nature's own jesters, an unspoken band.
So come join the ruckus, let humor take flight,
In a world where the silly shines ever so bright!

Crescendo of Blossoms and Beyond

Petals are pirouetting, twirling with flair,
A flower ballet, with none a care.
They hustle and bustle, like kids on the street,
While sunshine giggles, 'You're light on your feet!'

A daffodil teases, 'I'm the top of the crop!'
While daisies in chorus sing, 'Don't ever stop!'
With bees as their band, they sway in a line,
Every blossom a note, in nature's design.

'What was that noise?' asked the tulips in shock,
'Was that the sound of a rock or a sock?'
They peeked through their petals, just a bit shy,
'It's just a lost shoe. Don't worry, oh my!'

So here in the garden, the lunacy grows,
Where laughter and blooms flood the sun-kissed rows.
A crescendo erupts, let the joy never cease,
For in this wild whimsy, we find our release!

Petal-Laden Dreams Unfold

Among the green hues, where dreams are spun,
Petals are plotting a prankish run.
'Let's hide the gardener's hat!' one did propose,
While others held tight to a ticklish rose.

In this realm of green, everything is quirky,
The radish rebels get slightly berserk-y.
They nudge one another, 'Let's dance in the rain!'
While lettuce just whimpers, 'You'll ruin my grain!'

A chubby caterpillar munches on leaves,
'These are quite tasty, better than peas!'
With a chuckle, he quips, 'I dream of a spread,
A feast fit for kings, all buttery bread!'

So come join these dreams, where laughter takes root,
In petals of whimsy, life's wonderfully cute.
With every bright blossom, joy flows from the earth,
In this place of enchantment, we find our rebirth!

In the Heart of Greenery

In a garden bright, where the laughter grows,
Gnomes dance in hats with their bulbous noses.
Birds wear tuxedos, oh what a sight!
They chirp the tunes of a fruit-filled night.

Rabbits in boots hop from tree to tree,
Debating the best spot for a honey spree.
Squirrels chuckle as they race and slide,
Chasing their tails with no place to hide.

Every pumpkin grins, each carrot sings,
Whispering jokes of fantastical things.
Who knew that peppers could tickle your toes?
With laughter and joy, the whole garden glows!

So gather your friends, bring snacks to share,
In this merry place without a single care.
For in this green heart, the fun never ends,
With giggles and glee, all nature sends!

Shadows Cast by Ancient Roots

Beneath the boughs of tangled lore,
Lies a joker tree with a belly to roar.
It tickles the ground with its leafy jest,
While squirrels debate who can hop the best!

Caterpillars waltz on a slippery vine,
Sporting top hats, oh, how they shine!
With every twist and every turn,
They spin tales that make the mushrooms yearn!

Loud giggles echo through the leafy maze,
As apples conspire in mischievous ways,
They tumble and roll, just for fun,
Chasing down shadows in the afternoon sun!

With each crunch beneath calloused feet,
Nature's chuckle becomes a delightful beat.
Roots laugh aloud, a playful brigade,
In this tangled realm where joy is laid!

Chronicles of a Fruitful Haven

In a land where pears wear polka dots,
And the strawberries dance in silly spots.
Cherries form bands with rhythms sublime,
Making music in perfect time!

Plums play hide-and-seek among the vines,
While whispering secrets of sunny designs.
Watermelons roll with a hearty cheer,
As the sun winks down, oh, what a year!

Bananas slip by in a graceful sweep,
Tickling the roots where the rabbits creep.
Quirky outfits on every sprout,
Who knew a broccoli could twirl about?

This cheerful place with laughter and light,
Serves piecing laughter as a tasty bite.
So join the fun, come take your part,
In this fruitful haven that captures the heart!

The Allure of Starlit Branches

Under twinkling lights in the cool of night,
Berries wear shades, oh what a sight!
Hanging like jewels, they giggle and sway,
In this funny fruit tale, come laugh and play!

With lemons wearing jackets, and limes in bows,
They host a party where anything goes!
Tangerines tango, while grapes offer cheese,
Unlikely mates in this fruit-filled breeze.

Fireflies join with their flickering dance,
As everyone pairs up in a whimsy romance.
Pineapples crown their hilarious fest,
Crowning the night with an optimistic jest!

So raise a toast to this bubbly scene,
With laughter and joy woven in green.
For every branch holds a merry delight,
In this land of wonders, love shines bright!